St David's FOUNDATION

About St. David's Foundation

St. David's Foundation is one of the largest health foundations in the United States, funding over $100 million annually in a five-county area surrounding Austin, Texas. Through a unique partnership with St. David's HealthCare, the Foundation strategically reinvests proceeds from the hospital system back into the community, with a goal of advancing health equity and removing barriers to health for communities facing the greatest health needs.

About Via Hope

Via Hope Texas (Mental Health Resource Texas) originated as a component of the Texas' Mental Health Transformation Grant awarded by the Substance Abuse and Mental Health Services Administration (SAMHSA). Via Hope promotes wellness and recovery through peer support training, workforce development and organizational change work. They envision a world where lived experience is valued within systems & communities.

Acknowledgments

We are grateful to the library directors, library staff, and peer specialists who participated in L4H and shared their experiences with us, particularly those who provided early feedback on this toolkit during the November 2024 L4H convening. We are grateful to SDF for making L4H possible, especially Abena Asante, who led the development and implementation of the L4H program and whose efforts made this project possible. We also thank SDF team members Emily Burgess and Jesse Simmons for their insights and partnership throughout. We thank Christina Carney of Via Hope for her partnership and commitment to the L4H project. We also thank the Tocker Foundation for its guidance in the early development of L4H, Kathryn (Kit) Matthew of AEA Consulting, and the members of the Library Advisory Board for sharing their expertise and guidance throughout. This toolkit was substantially improved after integrating the thoughtful feedback from Monique Martineau (RAND) and our two quality assurance reviewers, Eunice Wong (RAND) and Melinda Hodges (library director at the Buda Public Library, an L4H-participating library).

AF854137

TOOLKIT

Supporting Community Mental Health in Libraries

A Toolkit for Implementing Evidence-Based Approaches

AMY L. SHEARER | IVY TODD | KAREN CHRISTIANSON | YOSELÍN MAYORAL
LOGAN DICK | RAJEEV RAMCHAND | SANDRA SMITH
TA'KISHA MOORE | LYNSAY AYER

RAND viaHOPE

For more information on this publication, visit www.rand.org/t/TLA3597-1.

About RAND

RAND is a research organization that develops solutions to public policy challenges to help make communities throughout the world safer and more secure, healthier and more prosperous. RAND is nonprofit, nonpartisan, and committed to the public interest. To learn more about RAND, visit www.rand.org.

Research Integrity

Our mission to help improve policy and decisionmaking through research and analysis is enabled through our core values of quality and objectivity and our unwavering commitment to the highest level of integrity and ethical behavior. To help ensure our research and analysis are rigorous, objective, and nonpartisan, we subject our research publications to a robust and exacting quality-assurance process; avoid both the appearance and reality of financial and other conflicts of interest through staff training, project screening, and a policy of mandatory disclosure; and pursue transparency in our research engagements through our commitment to the open publication of our research findings and recommendations, disclosure of the source of funding of published research, and policies to ensure intellectual independence. For more information, visit www.rand.org/about/research-integrity.

RAND's publications do not necessarily reflect the opinions of its research clients and sponsors.

Published by the RAND Corporation, Santa Monica, Calif.

© 2025 St. David's Foundation

RAND® is a registered trademark.

Photo Credits

Photos: Bookshelf—Liz Moskowitz, butterfly line drawing—Olga Rai / Adobe Stock; pp. iii, vi, 2, 5, 6, 15, 24, 42, 52, 58: Liz Moskowitz; p. 13: DMP/Getty Images; p. 34: SDI Productions / Getty Images; p. 18: golero / Getty Images. **Illustrations**: pp. v, 59: MD OMAR FARUK / Getty Images; pp. 1, 25, 53: Olga Rai / Adobe Stock; pp. 7, 35: Olena Kovrigo / Getty Images; pp. 19, 43: Sviatlana Herasimenka / Getty Images; p. 47: Tetiana Garkusha / Getty Images. **Icons**: implementation: sdecoret / Adobe Stock; checklist: sdecoret / Adobe Stock; tips: sdecoret / Adobe Stock; worksheet: sdecoret / Adobe Stock.

"The Libraries for Health program is bringing the mental health access to where the people are already gathered, where they are already looking for resources, and exploring services. That place is the public library. It is a community service institution by all means."

About This Toolkit

This toolkit provides instructions, ideas, and guidance to libraries that are interested in adopting mental health supports into their settings. It largely draws on lessons learned from Libraries for Health (L4H), a pilot program funded by St. David's Foundation (SDF) in which ten libraries in rural central Texas worked to embed mental health supports in their communities by targeting adult patrons. In January 2022, SDF contracted RAND to codesign, coordinate, and evaluate the program along with Via Hope, a central Texas–based nonprofit that provides peer training support and oversees the implementation of L4H. Findings from the evaluation will be published in summer 2025.

The toolkit is designed to help librarians identify and implement mental health supports within the library to support their patrons' mental well-being. The toolkit starts with a description of the rationale for incorporating mental health supports in libraries (Chapter 1) and a summary of how libraries approached this in the L4H pilot (Chapter 2). The remainder of the toolkit is intended to help guide librarians through the steps of successfully adding new mental health supports within their library environments. The development of this toolkit was envisioned and funded by St. David's Foundation.

Community Health and Environmental Policy Program

RAND Social and Economic Well-Being is a division of RAND that seeks to actively improve the health and social and economic well-being of populations and communities throughout the world. This research was conducted in the Community Health and Environmental Policy Program within RAND Social and Economic Well-Being. The program focuses on such topics as infrastructure, science and technology, industrial policy, community design, community health promotion, migration and population dynamics, transportation, energy, and climate and the environment, as well as other policy concerns that are influenced by the natural and built environment, technology, and community organizations and institutions that affect well-being. For more information, email chep@rand.org.

CONTENTS

MARTINDALE
TX
HCWC

CHAPTER 1

Introduction

This chapter provides an overview of the toolkit's purpose and how best to use it. This toolkit is a product of Libraries for Health (L4H), a pilot program that supported ten libraries in central Texas in embedding mental health supports in their libraries. We start by explaining how L4H came to be and what the program entailed. Next, we briefly describe who this toolkit is intended for: librarians and library staff who are interested in embedding mental health supports in their libraries. Finally, we describe how to use this toolkit and offer a preview of the included resources.

Embedding Mental Health Supports in Libraries

This toolkit draws from L4H, a mental health pilot program that aims to build community capacity for mental health and well-being by embedding mental health support in public libraries. L4H emerged from a partnership among St. David's Foundation (SDF), RAND, Via Hope, and ten public libraries in central Texas, in response to critical mental health needs and a shortage of mental health care providers. In collaboration with members of this partnership, we developed this toolkit to share lessons learned in the L4H pilot and to help other libraries successfully embed mental health supports within their unique setting.

Libraries occupy a unique place in American life: They are free community spaces that draw in a wide variety of community members. Although libraries' missions historically have focused on providing access to information, many libraries have expanded their scope to offer additional resources to their communities, such as computer and internet access, food bank programming, and language and literacy

“I was the one that introduced my sister and my sister-in-law [to the peer specialist]. And then as I saw the changes, especially on my sister, how she looked better . . . you see someone almost on a daily basis and see how their lifestyle was versus how they have changed now, it’s just—it’s working, it’s working.”

L4H library patron participant

classes. Libraries tend to be trusted and welcoming spaces in which individuals from diverse backgrounds access valuable programs and resources at no cost. Therefore, embedding mental health support into library programming can feel like a natural fit in many settings, especially for communities with growing mental health needs and a lack of traditional mental health resources.

L4H provided a peer specialist embedded in each participating library, funds for libraries to build mental health programming and resources, regular cohort gatherings, and trainings for the ten participating libraries to build their mental health knowledge and skills. Via Hope, a Texas-based nonprofit organization, trained and supervised the L4H peer specialists, facilitated the library cohort trainings, and provided technical assistance to L4H libraries. Because the cohort structure might not be easy for libraries to create outside a funded initiative, we do not discuss it in this toolkit. However, our full evaluation report (expected in summer 2025) will include findings pertaining to all aspects of L4H (Ayer et al., 2025).

The inclusion of lay mental health workers in each library addresses (1) a known shortage of mental health providers that affects communities nationwide and (2) a wealth of research showing that the stigma about seeking mental health support is a major deterrent to getting help (Health Resources and Services Administration, undated). L4H leverages these lay mental health workers by using a *task-sharing* approach to build capacity for and reduce barriers to community mental health care access. Task-sharing involves training lay people to provide mental health support, identify needs for additional assessment and treatment (e.g., therapy or medication), and provide a *warm handoff* to mental health providers when appropriate. In the case of L4H, peer specialists—i.e., individuals with lived experience of mental health challenges who use their training and experience to support others—fill the lay mental health worker role. Peer specialists practice active listening and advocacy, help people access the resources they need, help set personal recovery goals, share resources and provide education, and lead support groups, among other mental health activities. In regions with mental health provider shortages, peer specialists can reduce mental health providers' workload. They also can reduce individual barriers to accessing mental health treatment. Chapter 2 of this toolkit discusses peer specialist support in more detail. Although peer support and other task-sharing approaches have been used in various settings (e.g., emergency rooms, homeless shelters, jails), they have not, to our knowledge, been implemented in library settings prior to this project.

Even before peer specialists were fully integrated into their libraries, library staff played a pivotal role in kicking off L4H implementation by proactively initiating mental health activities. Staff recognized the immediate needs of their communities and used the grant funding provided by L4H to expand their mental health programming and resources. They incorporated mental health topics into existing library events, such as community health fairs and family story times, creating an inclusive environment that gently introduced patrons to mental health concepts. Additionally, library staff organized mental health–focused workshops and support groups, such as stress reduction classes and book clubs discussing mental health themes. These activities were often facilitated by library staff, community volunteers, or external facilitators, ensuring that the library remained a supportive and welcoming space for all patrons. By expanding their collections with mental health materials and resources, library staff further reinforced their commitment to addressing the mental health needs of their communities, demonstrating the library's role as a vital community resource, even in the absence of direct peer support. Library staff also benefited directly from training that built their mental health competency and their ability to respond to patrons in need.

More information about the L4H pilot, including news articles and a photo essay, can be found at https://stdavidsfoundation.org/how-we-work/grantmaking/what-we-fund/thriving-rural-communities/libraries-for-health/ (SDF, undated).

How to Use This Tool

Intended Audience

This toolkit provides ideas, instructions, and tools to library directors and staff who wish to integrate mental health supports into their settings. Directors and staff can use this toolkit to set goals, establish partnerships, and plan implementation processes. Organizations that wish to support libraries in their mental health integration efforts (for example, through funding or coordination support) might also benefit from this toolkit.

We imagine that library leaders (such as directors or staff with management responsibility) will most often spearhead the steps we outline in this toolkit. However, we recommend completing the steps and worksheets in collaboration with other project stakeholders as they come on board. These stakeholders might include library staff who will be involved in implementation, staff from any partnering organizations, and the library's peer specialist, if you recruit one.

Navigating the Toolkit

The chapters in this toolkit provide detailed guidance for anyone who would like to replicate components of L4H in their library. The process for planning and launching L4H outlined in this toolkit closely aligns with the evidence-based Getting To Outcomes™ (GTO) process, tailored for libraries.[1] We adapted the GTO steps using insights shared with us from library staff, directors, and peer specialists who participated in L4H.

This toolkit contains several features to help implement L4H, and these features are signaled with corresponding signposts.

- Worksheets to help you organize, reflect, and plan your work. We recommend not skipping these.
- Checklists to help you track all the recommended components of a step.
- Tip sheets to help you locate useful resources for effective L4H planning and implementation.
- Implementation examples from L4H pilot libraries, which can serve as inspiration during the planning process.

An annex to this toolkit, with editable versions of the worksheets, is available at www.rand.org/t/TLA3597-1.

We encourage libraries considering L4H to follow the steps as outlined in the toolkit. However, depending on the library's existing capacity, resources, and partnerships, the library director and staff may pursue the steps in a different order from the outline in this tool. They might also need to revisit or iterate on these steps as they move forward in the planning process, especially if new partnerships need to be developed.

This toolkit serves as a comprehensive guide for libraries aiming to integrate mental health supports into their environments, drawing on insights from the L4H pilot program. This chapter introduces the rationale behind incorporating mental health supports in libraries and provides guidance on how to use the tool effectively. Chapter 2 delves into the components of L4H, including lay mental health workers, peer support, programming, activities, and external partnerships. In Chapter 3, libraries are guided through assessing their readiness and capacity to adopt L4H, and we offer strategies to enhance both. Chapter 4 focuses on identifying community needs and setting programming goals, while Chapter 5 helps libraries select specific L4H activities, such as finding peer specialists and choosing suitable mental health activities. Chapter 6 outlines the preparation and launch phase, emphasizing the importance of building partnerships, securing funding, and creating a detailed workplan. Chapter 7 provides strategies for continuous improvement and sustaining L4H initiatives over time. Finally, Chapter 8 concludes the toolkit, summarizing the journey and reinforcing the commitment to supporting patrons' mental well-being.

---

[1] GTO is an evidence-based process for implementing, evaluating, and improving community programs. More than two decades of research have shown that programs that use the process are more likely to achieve their intended outcomes (RAND Corporation, undated).

UNDERSTANDING MENTAL ILLNESS
10 Things Everyone Should Know About
Bipolar Disorder
HAPPY
SAD
ANGRY
EMPTY
INVINCIBLE
INERT
GET THE FACTS
Depression
Let's Talk About It
Nutrition &
Your Mental Health
MUCH BETTER MOOD AHEAD
KEFIR
PROTECT YOUR HEALTH
How Stress Affects Your Health
(and what you can do about it!)
STRESS-O-METER
LOWER YOUR STRESS
SURGEON GENERAL'S REPORT
36 THINGS
EVERYONE SHOULD KNOW ABOUT
ADDICTION
AN EASY-TO-READ SUMMARY
Suicide
30 Facts Everyone Should Know
1. On average, there are 130 suicides per day in the U.S.
2. The rate of suicide is highest in adults between ages 45 and 64.
3. There is no single cause for suicide.

and into the
library I go to
lose my mind
and find
my soul

CHAPTER 2

Topics covered in this chapter:

- Peer support in libraries
- Mental health programming and activities for libraries
- External partnerships and resources

Resources included:

Implementation Examples: Libraries for Health Peer Specialist Activities

Tip Sheet: Peer Specialist Responsibilities—Do's and Don'ts

Libraries for Health Components

This chapter details three core components of L4H: peer specialists, mental health activities, and supportive partnerships. Peer specialists—the lay mental health workers who were trained to offer mental health resources and support to fellow adult community members—formed the foundation of L4H. Libraries also supplemented their L4H program with mental health activities, including programming for patrons and staff, and established supportive partnerships with other libraries and community organizations.

Peer Support in Libraries

Previous research has demonstrated the effectiveness of training community members to build capacity for mental health support and remove barriers for individuals in need of treatment (Barnett et al., 2018; Magidson et al., 2019; Snell-Rood and Schoenberg, 2019). These lay mental health workers can leverage cultural competence, existing relationships, and trust built with community members to deliver evidence-based mental health strategies to reach individuals who might not access mental health supports otherwise. Training typically involves ways to identify or screen for mental health concerns and then deploy evidence-based strategies to reduce symptoms and connect individuals with other services, if needed (e.g., mental health evaluation or treatment). Lay mental health workers can take on formal roles, such as community health workers, doulas, or peer specialists in health care settings. Alternatively, staff in community-based settings, such as barbers, tattoo artists, librarians, or workforce development staff, can be trained as lay mental health workers. To learn more about these different models of community-based mental health support, we recommend reading the Bipartisan Policy Center's January 2023 report, *Filling the Gaps in the Behavioral Health Workforce* (Gilbert et al., 2023).

After considering multiple program-design options, L4H ultimately selected peer specialists as the ideal type of lay mental health worker for delivering mental health support to adult library patrons. Peer specialists are individuals who have lived experience with mental health challenges and have experienced success in navigating these challenges. L4H used Via Hope to train peer specialists to listen to patrons, share their own experiences, and offer support and resources to help address patrons' struggles.

L4H selected the peer specialist role for three main reasons. First, initial conversations with libraries showed that although library staff viewed mental health support as a priority, they also felt overwhelmed with their existing tasks and would be reluctant to take on additional mental health responsibilities, including the supervision of peer support. Thus, sustainable, low-cost options for bringing lay mental health workers into the libraries were needed, as opposed to training the library staff in how to implement mental health strategies.

Second, peer support has evolved over time to become a widely recognized evidence-based practice for improving the mental health and well-being of individuals in a variety of settings and contexts. These include adults with serious mental illness, individuals with dual histories of incarceration and mental illness, socially isolated and lower-income older adults, youth and adolescents coping with loneliness and isolation, individuals with disabilities, families and caregivers of individuals with mental illness, and medically and socially disadvantaged populations (Shalaby and Agyapong, 2020). However, even though peer specialists have been operating in varied settings, to our knowledge, they had not previously been used in a library setting.

Finally, state-certified peer support had become newly reimbursable through Medicaid in Texas (Texas Medicaid and Healthcare Partnership, 2020). Peer specialists were fully funded by SDF for the L4H pilot, but the new reimbursement process gave a potential avenue for libraries to sustain peer support after the SDF-funded L4H project ended.

Peer Support Activities in the Pilot

Peer specialists took on a variety of responsibilities in the L4H pilot libraries (Table 2.1). Most commonly, L4H peer specialists provided one-on-one mental health support and connected patrons to resources. This occurred through drop-in office hours or scheduled appointments, as well as through being available at events to meet and talk with patrons. Peer specialists might help patrons find mental health providers, schedule appointments, complete paperwork, and talk through their mental health goals. They can provide social support and general encouragement and advice for anyone experiencing a mental health challenge or stressor.

Within the L4H pilot, most peer specialists also planned and led mental health activities, either to engage hard-to-reach populations or to provide direct mental health education and support, as needed. Such activities included support groups, mental health–related book groups, community resource fairs, and wellness activities and workshops.

L4H peer specialists also provided support to staff. One way this occurred was through a *warm handoff*, a direct person-to-person process that allowed library staff to seamlessly transfer addressing the mental

Table 2.1 | Implementation Examples: Libraries for Health Peer Specialist Activities

Peer Specialist Activities	Examples
Provided one-on-one support to patrons	• General wellness and emotional support • Assistance with accessing food, clothing, services, and transportation • Help with obtaining documentation (e.g., driver's license) or applying for public benefits (e.g., Supplemental Nutrition Assistance Program [SNAP], Medicaid)
Led new wellness programming and/or augmented existing programming for patrons	• Mental health–focused book clubs • Support groups for those experiencing anxiety, depression, grief, and/or challenges with parenting • Mental health classes • Social events
Supported library staff	• Mental health–focused book clubs • Support groups for those experiencing anxiety, depression, grief, and/or challenges with parenting • Mental health classes • Social events • Emotional support • Recommendations for how to interact with patrons experiencing mental health challenges
Identified and built connections with community partners; served as mental health resource liaison	• Creation of local resource directories • Establishment of local organizations
Supported staff with general library tasks to build familiarity and trust with patrons	• Participation in existing, non–mental health programming • Circulation desk assistance and help with both general and technology questions, as a way of introduction to patrons as peer specialists

health needs of a patron to the peer specialist. This process reduced the burden on library staff and allowed them to focus on more-standard library tasks. Peer specialists also directly supported staff by sharing information on how to support patrons experiencing mental health challenges, debriefing with staff who experienced challenging patron encounters, and providing support to staff who had their own need for mental health support.

Many L4H peer specialists also identified and built connections with local community organizations and leaders (e.g., homeless shelters, veterans' groups, mental health organizations, sheriffs). Peer specialists sometimes compiled these organizations into a community resource list for staff to share with patrons. When needed, peer specialists also connected patrons directly to their contacts at these organizations by providing a warm handoff.

Finally, L4H peer specialists also supported general library operations to build familiarity and trust with patrons. Peer specialists built these relationships by attending existing programming centered on mental health and by helping answer patrons' questions at the circulation desk.

"[Our peer specialists] both do . . . office hours for a couple of hours each week where people could sign up to come meet with them, one-on-one. One does a twice-monthly anxiety and depression support group, and then the other does a weekly, we call it, calm crafting. . . . They also do a mental help book club and a neurodiverse peer support group."

L4H library director

The following tip sheet provides a quick overview of what peer specialist roles typically do and do not involve.

Tip Sheet: Peer Specialist Roles—Do's and Don'ts

Peer specialists do . . .

- Deliver emotional and social support to patrons and staff
- Advocate for patrons to access mental health support
- Educate on mental health resources
- Build partnerships with local mental health resources
- Serve as a warm handoff for staff to refer patrons experiencing mental health challenges
- Lead support groups and mental health workshops
- Help patrons connect with additional mental health–related resources and navigate the local mental health system of care
- Plan mental health activities with staff and community partners

Peer specialists typically do not . . .

- Check circulation materials in or out, without also offering peer support activities
- Solely provide reference desk support that is general in nature or unrelated to mental health, without also offering peer support activities
- Plan library offerings that are unrelated to mental health
- Provide clinical counseling (e.g., therapy)
- Diagnose mental health conditions
- Enroll patients in clinical trials

"I do a lot of one-on-one interviews where I just let people talk to me about their lives and let them vent because a lot of people just need someone to talk to."

L4H peer specialist

Certification and Supervision

Peer support requires a set of skills that can be developed and enhanced through specialized trainings. Peer specialist training and certification programs are available in many states, both in person and virtually (Chapter 6 provides more information). Peer training and certification programs include the following:

- **Recovery Support Peer Specialist.** Individuals with lived experience of substance use recovery provide empathetic support, share recovery strategies, and guide others in their journey to recovery.
- **Mental Health Peer Specialist.** Individuals with personal experience of mental health challenges develop their skills in empathy, active listening, and the provision of practical guidance to support others in their mental health recovery.
- **Reentry Peer Specialist.** Individuals who have experienced the reentry process offer support, resources, and guidance to those transitioning from incarceration to community life.
- **Peer Support Supervisor.** Individuals learn to effectively manage and support peer support staff, ensuring high-quality assistance for individuals in recovery or dealing with mental health challenges.

To become certified as a peer specialist in Texas, an individual must attend a three-day core training and a five-day supplemental training. After completing a Federal Bureau of Investigation background check, the newly trained peer specialist can then apply for their six-month initial certification. Once approved, they must accumulate 250 supervised hours of practice. Upon completion of the 250 hours, the peer specialist can then apply for their full two-year certification. In other states, interested individuals can participate in peer support trainings and earn certification (if available) through the entities listed in the Substance Abuse and Mental Health Services Administration (SAMHSA) Peer Recovery Organizations state certification database (see Center for Addiction Recovery Support, undated) or the Copeland Center Peer Specialist Database (see Copeland Center for Wellness and Recovery, undated).

Peer specialists are supervised by a certified peer specialist supervisor, who supports and guides the peer specialist through and after the certification process. Peer specialist supervisors use a strengths-based, person-centered, trauma-informed approach, which leverages individuals' capabilities, prioritizes their

"Peer support really is just: I am here to support my peers, however, they need it, in the best way I can."

L4H peer specialist

unique needs and involvement, and integrates trauma sensitivity. The supervisor oversees and coaches the peer specialist in their delivery of peer services. They also conduct weekly one-on-one or group supervision sessions, either in person or via teleconference, that focus on skill-building, ethical problem-solving, professional growth strategies, and role clarity, as well as discussing the peer specialist's service delivery and activities. Topics specific to the peer specialist's site, such as organizational policies and other administrative matters, might be addressed as well. Peer specialist supervisors identify and address any issues or challenges that arise and help ensure that peer specialists adhere to ethical and professional standards. A peer specialist supervisor can also act as a role model, change agent, mentor, advocate, cheerleader, and motivator for the peer specialist.

Mental Health Programming and Activities

In addition to employing a peer specialist, L4H libraries hosted a wide variety of mental health programming. Libraries, along with their peer specialist and community partners, can tailor these activities according to the needs and preferences of their patrons. Activities can be led by peer specialists, qualified facilitators, library staff, and community volunteers. Most commonly, L4H libraries

- incorporated mental health topics and peer specialists into existing programming
- hosted mental health–focused workshops and groups
- expanded their mental health materials and resources.

In this section, we provide a bit more detail about what these different types of programing can resemble.

Incorporating Mental Health Topics and Peer Specialists into Programming

The stigma around mental health prevents many individuals from seeking support (Arnaez et al., 2020; Schnyder et al., 2017). L4H was implemented in rural Texas, and many participating library directors noted that patrons were unlikely to engage in programming if it was labeled as "mental health" or to engage with a peer specialist with whom they were unfamiliar. These directors felt that, as a starting point, incorporating the peer specialist into existing programming could help introduce patrons to the idea of accessing peer support and mental health programming from the library, decrease the stigma associated with these activities, and develop trust and familiarity with the peer specialist. Sometimes, these initial steps included incorporating

mental health topics into activities that were already serving patrons, particularly those patrons who might be deterred by an activity that appeared to be focused on mental health. In L4H, these activities included

- community health fairs that introduced the peer specialist and showcased community mental health resources along with other types of health services in the area
- mobile book deliveries, attended by the peer specialist
- family story times or movie nights, during which the peer specialist met and mingled with adult patrons
- special-interest activities—such as crafting, gardening, or tabletop games—that often included mental health topics or themes and were designed to encourage and give patrons a calming environment in which to engage socially and become familiar with the peer specialist
- group meetings or activities for special populations—such as lesbian, gay, bisexual, transgender, queer-plus (LGBTQ+) patrons; caregivers; or seniors—with general support or mental health–focused topics.

Although these activities can be effective in engaging specific target populations, these activities would not be expected to achieve noticeable improvements in individual mental health–related outcomes, such as reduced mental health symptoms or improved well-being. Libraries should consider pairing these activities with peer support and other evidence-based mental health support and education activities.

Hosting Mental Health–Focused Programming and Groups

In addition to adding mental health topics into existing programming, L4H libraries implemented new programming geared to support and educate patrons on specific mental health topics. Examples included

- book clubs that selected books to spark conversations about mental health
- yoga events to introduce mindfulness topics and provide stress-reducing physical activity
- stress reduction classes
- support groups for people caring for others (e.g., parents, caregivers) or experiencing grief, anxiety, and depression.

Libraries that implement mental health programming to meet the needs of their patron population would do so, ideally, in conjunction with their peer specialist, who can plan, coordinate, or lead these activities. However, activities also can be implemented by community partners or hired facilitators from mental health organizations.

Mental health programming and activities need not only focus on patron mental health; they also can support the mental and emotional well-being of library staff. As public-facing employees, library staff face stressors related to challenging interactions or secondary trauma (i.e., mental health symptoms stemming from hearing about the traumatic experiences of others).

The
Library
is
OPEN

More examples and tips on where to find evidence-based community interventions can be found in Chapter 5.

Mental Health Materials and Resources

Libraries also can augment their collections with mental health materials and lists of local resources and referrals. A peer specialist can provide recommendations for reliable and accurate books and audiovisual materials, as well as accompanying resource lists. Examples include

- books and authors that cover mental health topics in non-stigmatizing ways
- mental health kits that feature wellness materials, activities, or resources, such as a yoga kit with information on mindfulness and relaxation, a yoga mat, and DVDs or digital downloads of yoga tutorials
- community mental health resource guides.

External Partnerships and Resources

Libraries can benefit from partnerships with community organizations or providers that serve individuals with mental health needs, either directly with mental health care or indirectly with housing, employment, transportation, or other types of support. Many of the L4H pilot libraries expanded their community partnerships during L4H. These partnerships can be invaluable for mental health support activities, such as conducting a comprehensive needs and resources assessment (as outlined in Chapter 4), cataloging information to create a resource guide, implementing partner activities and trainings, and assisting patrons in need as they seek additional mental health support. Examples of ways to use partnerships to promote mental health within libraries include the following:

- **Asking a community partner to host a class or series related to mental health.** For example, a local yoga instructor could host a weekly yoga class, or someone from the local American Legion could host a series on veterans' mental health.
- **Engaging a community partner to train staff on how to engage with patrons who are experiencing mental health challenges.** This might include tips on how to de-escalate patrons who are upset and provide warm handoffs to mental health providers and other services in the community.
- **Establishing a partnership with a mental health provider or social service provider to colocate in a library space (e.g., embedding a social worker).** This requires, at a minimum, developing a partnership with a mental health provider and finding a physical space in the library.

Which community partners you decide to engage will depend on your community's needs, program goals, and activity selection, as well as the availability of partnering organizations.

Before launching a new partnership, it is important to consider what role each person will play in that partnership. Table 2.2 outlines the distinct and overlapping responsibilities of library staff, lay mental health workers, and community partners who are trying to work together to support patrons' mental health.

Before diving into hiring a peer specialist, planning programming, and developing partnerships, we highly recommend that you first assess your library's readiness and capacity to implement L4H, as described in Chapter 3.

Table 2.2 | Responsibilities of Library Staff, Peer Specialists, and Community Partners

Goal	Library Staff	Peer Specialists	Community Partners
Build relationships	Build relationships with local community organizations and with the peer specialist and include them in library planning meetings.	Build relationships with library staff, local mental health providers, and community organizations.	Build relationships with the library.
Host mental health–focused programming	Integrate mental health topics into library operations and programs.	Develop, lead, or support library programming with a mental health focus.	If needed, lead library programming on specialized topics that require more expertise, such as formal support groups.
Compile and share community resources	Provide patrons with resources and information about mental health resources and support.	Develop resource guides; provide patrons with information about mental health resources and support patrons as they navigate them.	Educate staff, peer specialists, and patrons about the resources you offer.
Provide support to patrons in need	Learn and use new mental health skills for patron interactions and crisis management (e.g., mental health first aid, suicide prevention).	Provide direct emotional support and encouragement to patrons, when appropriate.	Provide clinical care to patrons needing mental health treatment.
Refer patrons, as needed	Facilitate patron connections with peer specialist or mental health partners.	Help patrons access mental health providers when clinical care is warranted, including a warm handoff and follow-up.	If needed, adapt policies to provide service to referred patrons.
Reduce mental health stigma	Reduce stigma surrounding mental health through education and events.	Reduce stigma surrounding mental health through sharing personal experience.	Share data and stories librarians can use to help reduce stigma around mental health.

CHAPTER 3

Topics covered in this chapter:

- Assess your library's readiness to take on new programming
- Check your organization's current capacity for L4H implementation specifically
- Plan to build readiness and capacity before launch

Resources included:

- Checklist: Assessing Readiness
- Tip Sheet: Estimated Resource Intensity of Mental Health Support Activities
- Worksheet: Assessing Capacity to Implement Libraries for Health

Readiness and Capacity for Libraries for Health

This chapter is designed to help you assess whether your library has sufficient readiness and capacity to launch L4H. As with any new program, it is important to assess organizational readiness before jumping in. Readiness assessment is a process that requires reflecting on your library's current scope of work, level of resources, and bandwidth to take on something new. If you find that your organization is not ready to take on new programming, consider what needs to change to become ready.

Assess Readiness

L4H requires libraries to devote time and resources to plan, launch, and implement new programming. Before taking on new programming, first consider whether your library can adequately meet **existing** obligations (see the following checklist).

Checklist: Assessing Readiness

Does your library have:

- ☐ Adequate, stable staffing to meet existing obligations?
- ☐ Adequate, stable funding to meet existing obligations?

If you answered "no" to either of these questions, we recommend building these resources before trying to add new programming. This might involve seeking additional resources, such as library funding, additional staff, or a volunteer group. If staffing is not adequate to meet existing obligations, consider whether any activities, tasks, or job duties could be deprioritized in favor of a focus on new mental health programs.

If your library is adequately staffed and funded to meet existing obligations, consider next whether your library is ready to take on additional obligations.

Check Capacity for Implementation

Introducing a new initiative, such as L4H, presents an exciting opportunity to enhance the library's role in community well-being and support. As with any new initiative, L4H involves new tasks and potentially increased workload for staff. By thoughtfully integrating L4H, library staff and stakeholders can experience a renewed sense of purpose and engagement, leading to a more dynamic and fulfilling work environment. Ensuring that staff workloads are balanced and manageable is key to maintaining high morale and productivity. When staff feel supported and empowered, they are better equipped to take on the challenge of new programming. By carefully thinking through required resources, prioritizing staff well-being, and offering the necessary resources and training, the library can create a thriving environment in which both employees and patrons benefit from the enriched services.

Some activities are going to require more resources, and some will require relatively fewer resources to implement. The following tip sheet ranks the resource intensity of various mental health support activities.

The following library capacities facilitated strong L4H implementation in the pilot libraries when present but posed implementation challenges when absent. We recommend that libraries that are considering L4H have or make plans to build the following capacity before starting new programs:

- **Initiative leader.** Libraries will need an internal L4H leader to spearhead the initiative, develop goals and plans, and coordinate activities. This person will take ownership of the various planning and preparation steps and take responsibility for moving the work forward. The leader does not need to work alone, but they will be responsible for delegating tasks.

Tip Sheet: Estimated Resource Intensity of Mental Health Support Activities at Your Library

Resource Intensity	Activities
LESS	Incorporating a mental health theme into existing library programming (e.g., choosing a mental health–themed book for book club or highlighting mental health book recommendations)
	Inviting local mental health organizations to promote their resources
	Inviting local mental health organizations to plan and host an event or activity
	Having staff attend a mental health training
	Planning one-off mental health activities (e.g., offering a mindfulness workshop)
	Planning ongoing mental health activities (e.g., weekly yoga and wellness classes)
	Colocating mental health services
	Offering multiple, ongoing mental health activities
	Sponsoring a staff or volunteer to become a certified peer specialist and offering peer support
	Hiring a peer specialist and offering peer support
MORE	Designating a staff or volunteer to coordinate and manage mental health programming

- **Staff time.** Library staff can contribute programming ideas, support planning and implementation, share information with patrons about peer support and other mental health resources, and welcome the peer specialist into the library. Staff in pilot libraries enjoyed opportunities to contribute their ideas and share their connections with community resources, but some library staff struggled to balance L4H with their existing work. Make sure that staff have room in their schedules to meaningfully contribute.
- **Access to additional financial resources.** Peer specialists were funded by SDF, and pilot libraries also received funding from SDF to attend staff trainings, expand collections, and build out mental health–related programming. Your library might not need additional financial resources to implement some of the less resource-intense activities (for example, highlighting existing mental health collections, incorporating mental health themes into existing programs, or partnering with mental health organizations that can provide resources). However, additional financial resources will enable your library to broaden its reach and expand mental health offerings. More information about funding mental health activities is provided in Chapter 6.

"The return has been great because it has opened up a new idea of what the library does in the community, who we serve, and what we are able to offer. It has brought in people who have previously not thought of the library in that way."

L4H library staff

- **Buy-in from organizational leadership and staff.** Organizational and leadership buy-in for mental health programming is essential for successful implementation. Taking on new programming requires organizational changes (e.g., to resource allocation or priorities). Such changes will be challenging without top-level support. It is also hard to implement these changes without the support of at least a few staff members, so make sure that they are also on board.
- **Connections to develop external partnerships** with community mental health resources and social services. Partnerships will be critical to understanding the available resources and unmet needs in your community. Building relationships with social service providers will expand your library's ability to share information about those resources with patrons. Relationship-building could also lead to referrals, opportunities for warm handoffs, and other ways to support the community.
- **Dedicated space(s)** for L4H programming. One-on-one peer support requires private, quiet spaces for confidentiality. Pilot libraries also benefitted from conference rooms or other event spaces for group programming. If your library does not currently have space available for L4H, consider ways to find or build such a space (for example, partnering with another organization or community center, starting a garden, or finding outdoor space).
- **Experience collecting and tracking engagement data.** Collecting information and feedback on L4H's reach and effectiveness can inform program improvements and support investments.

To help your library assess its capacity in these areas before launching L4H, complete the following "Assessing Capacity to Implement Libraries for Health" worksheet.

Plan to Build Readiness and Capacity

Ideally, your library would have answered "yes" to all questions on the "Assessing Capacity to Implement Libraries for Health" worksheet, but it likely had at least one "no," indicating a capacity that could be further developed. Although not all of these capacities need to be fully in place before launching—many of the pilot libraries did not have all of them in place—things will likely go smoother if the capacities are underway. If your library is falling short in a few areas, take time now to plan how to build those capacities.

For example, if your library does not currently have a private space for a peer specialist to support a patron, how could one be created? Perhaps there is an outdoor space, an office they can borrow for a few hours per day, a resource closet that could be repurposed, or an option for them to meet patrons out in the community.

Worksheet: Assessing Capacity to Implement Libraries for Health

Does your library have . . .	Yes / no	If yes: Describe the capacity. If no: Describe the steps that need to be taken to achieve this capacity.
An initiative leader—preferably with experience implementing library programming—who can coordinate and manage L4H?	Y ☐ N ☐	
Staff time and bandwidth for new programming?	Y ☐ N ☐	
Access to additional financial resources?	Y ☐ N ☐	
Leadership and staff buy-in for mental health programming?	Y ☐ N ☐	
Connections to develop external partnerships?	Y ☐ N ☐	
Available space(s) for L4H programming?	Y ☐ N ☐	
Systems in place to collect and track engagement data?	Y ☐ N ☐	

Regarding thinking through staff capacity: If staff are going to be asked to plan new programming, is there any existing programming that could be cut to prevent staff from being overburdened? Or perhaps your library could plan to have staff augment existing programming and to rely on your peer specialist or community partners to lead any new mental health–focused programming.

Once you do feel confident that your library is ready and has sufficient capacity to launch L4H, you are ready to proceed to the following chapters, which provide more detail on how to plan and implement. Turn to Chapter 4 for guidance on how to identify your community's mental health needs and set goals around challenges you are seeking to address through L4H.

Mental
Health Care
Balanced
Nutrition
Supportive
Relationships
Stress
Busters
Mindfulness
Practices
Quality
Sleep
Physical
Activity

CHAPTER 4

Topics covered in this chapter:

- Identifying community needs and resources
- Setting goals

Resources included:

- Implementation Example: Keeping Track of No's
- Checklist: Sources of Information on Community Needs
- Worksheet: Identifying and Prioritizing Community Needs and Resources
- Worksheet: Setting SMART Goals

Community Needs and Goal Setting

This chapter will help you identify your community's mental health needs and set goals for what you hope to accomplish through L4H. Assessing community needs before setting goals or implementing activities is crucial to ensuring that the activities address the specific challenges and priorities of your community. This approach optimizes resource allocation and increases the likelihood of successful outcomes by aligning your activities with the actual needs and cultural context of your target population.

A note about the order of planning and implementation: We recommend identifying community needs, setting goals, and *then* planning activities to meet those goals. This is a best practice in implementation science and will ensure that your planned activities directly tie back to your community needs. Hiring a peer specialist and choosing which activities to implement might depend on your ability to secure funding. Therefore, your library might choose to pursue funding before, during, or after these planning activities. More information about funding a peer specialist and mental health programming is in Chapter 6.

Implementation Example

Keeping Track of No's

To identify potential unmet community needs, one L4H pilot library started keeping track of each time staff had to tell a patron that "no," the library did not offer a particular program or service.

TIP: Write down occasions when patrons make requests or ask about services that your library does not currently offer, and consider whether these requests point to opportunities to expand library services.

Identify and Prioritize Community Needs and Resources

To design and provide mental health programming that will help patrons, libraries must first understand what types of help patrons need and what types of resources are already available. Conducting a needs-and-resources assessment involves gathering information from staff, community partners, and patrons. We know that finding this information is library staff's area of expertise. If possible, try to find the answer to the following questions:

- What are the specific mental health needs of library patrons? The broader community?
- Which populations experience these needs? How does this library setting engage with these populations?
- What resources already exist in this library or in the broader community to address these needs? To what extent do these resources meet patron needs?
- What barriers do patrons face in accessing those existing resources? Where do patrons experience gaps in available resources?
- What specific mental health needs of library patrons and community members are not currently being met?

Asking these questions is the first step to designing activities that will be meaningful to patrons and will help address gaps in the community. With a better understanding of community needs, your library can more effectively direct resources (such as time, funding, and energy) to where they can have the biggest impact on community mental health. Understanding the landscape of existing community service providers will also help your library identify potential partner organizations that might have similar goals and complementary resources.

To begin your needs and resources assessment, first consider the resources in the following checklist. Although patrons' acute needs might make themselves obvious, consider less visible mental health symptoms and needs experienced in your community (for example, loneliness and social isolation), and seek out additional sources of information or data to help

Checklist: Sources of Information on Community Needs

Are you able to locate data from these sources?	Yes / no	Notes
Existing local needs assessment of community mental health conducted by a local or regional hospital, university, or mental health care provider	Y ☐ N ☐	
Existing local community survey of mental health service needs or concerns, perhaps conducted by local government	Y ☐ N ☐	
Data on community needs from local community organizations (mental health advocacy and service provider organizations in your area might already be generating reports on community mental health needs and might be willing to share data with you)	Y ☐ N ☐	
Local community data from national sources, such as • U.S. Census demographic data about your community: https://data.census.gov/ (U.S. Census Bureau, undated) • Health Resources and Services Administration (HRSA) data on medically underserved areas and workforce shortages: https://data.hrsa.gov/topics/health-workforce/shortage-areas (HRSA, undated) • Mental Health America dashboard with levels of mental health need in your state and county based on their online screening survey: https://mhanational.org/mhamapping/mha-state-county-data (Mental Health America, undated) • Centers for Disease Control and Prevention PLACES interactive map and downloadable data from even communities of various sizes on the prevalence of dozens of different health conditions (including mental health): https://www.cdc.gov/places/ (Centers for Disease Control and Prevention, undated)	Y ☐ N ☐	
Mental health experts and professionals working in your community, including • local National Alliance on Mental Illness (NAMI) state organization or affiliate: https://www.nami.org/findsupport/ (NAMI, undated-a) • local Mental Health America affiliate: https://arc.mhanational.org/find-affiliate (Mental Health America Affiliate Resource Center, undated)	Y ☐ N ☐	
Feedback from patrons regarding their programming interests or satisfaction with any existing mental health offerings at the library	Y ☐ N ☐	

Worksheet: Identifying and Prioritizing Community Needs and Resources

Instructions: The goal of this worksheet is to identify opportunities for your library to intervene for impact. Review the data you have collected. Then, list each mental health need on a separate row (the second column provides an example below). Where resources exist to meet patron needs, consider whether your library can help connect patrons to those resources. Where resources do not exist or are insufficient to meet patron needs, consider the feasibility of developing programs or partnerships to fill this gap.

Prioritization Question	Example
What is the mental health challenge or need?	Loneliness and isolation
Response:	
Who is most affected by this issue (e.g., groups distinguished by shared ages, races, languages, interests, and/or experiences)?	This is a national trend, and we expect that many patrons experience loneliness. Local news reports have recently focused on isolation in seniors and older adults.
Response:	
What programs or services does the library currently offer to address this challenge?	Seniors frequent the library during the daytime and chat with library staff, but we do not have programming specifically for seniors.
Response:	
What other community resources exist to support this challenge or this population?	Local community centers offer exercise classes for seniors. The senior housing program offers some social activities, but they are only available to program residents.
Response:	

Prioritization Question	Example
What barriers does this population face to accessing these resources, either at the library or from other organizations?	No explicit senior activities in the library. Limited senior programming at community centers; costs might be prohibitive.
Response:	
What will be required to meet this need or address the barriers to existing resources (e.g., help patrons access existing resources, supplement existing resources, create new programs to address this need)?	• Socialization groups or opportunities that appeal to seniors, at times that work with their schedules and are free or very low cost. • Coordinated transportation to enable seniors in the community to attend.
Response:	
How challenging will it be for your library to gather the required resources to meet this need?	Minimally; we can easily plan programming, but coordinating transportation might be complex. We will have to reach out to different transportation services in the area as a first step to determine what is feasible.
Response:	
Is addressing this need a high, medium, or low priority? Consider whether the need is acute, urgent, or disruptive to library operations.	High
Response:	

identify other needs. Try to use information from at least two, but preferably three, different sources (such as reports from local organizations, American Community Survey data, and discussions with professionals) to triangulate the key issues. The more recent the data, the better; try to review data collected in the past five years.

Once you have information from multiple sources, review the data to identify trends that might indicate mental health needs within your community. Enter the information into the "Identifying and Prioritizing Community Needs and Resources" worksheet. If you identify multiple needs, you can use the worksheet to prioritize what to address first.

To prioritize needs, consider the urgency of the need, your library's access to the population experiencing the need, and what will be needed to address the barriers you identified. Think carefully and strategically about addressing needs for which your library might be uniquely positioned to contribute to community well-being. Although libraries can provide a wide variety of services to patrons, no library can meet every need of every patron. Taking on too broad of a scope or too many issues at once might lead to duplicative efforts with existing organizations, ineffective programming, or staff stress and burnout.

Set Goals for Programming

Next, set goals using the needs that you prioritized in the previous worksheet. Setting high-level goals for L4H upfront will help inform the activities you decide to implement and guide your efforts to develop partnerships and build capacity.

We recommend setting goals related to two or three needs you identified above. Use the "Setting SMART Goals" worksheet to set goals.

Once you have decided which mental health challenge(s) you would like to address through L4H, create a goal statement for the each of the prioritized needs you plan to address. Use the SMART acronym to help set strong goal statements—i.e., goals that are

- **S**pecific. Say what change is expected and for whom.
- **M**easurable. State the amount of change you expect or hope to see.
- **A**chievable. The goal should be realistic and attainable.
- **R**elevant. The goal should address the identified needs.
- **T**ime-bound. The goal should have a defined timeline by which the change is expected to occur.

"We are forming partnerships and determining which of the programs have had the greatest impact. With a combination of partnerships, additional grants, and city funding—we expect to maintain a source of mental health services to our community."

L4H library progress report

The *S*, *M*, and *T* components will go into your goal statement; the *A* and *R* components are logic checks to think about as you write your goal.

Your goal should always focus on a specific, malleable feature of the target population—i.e., something that is possible to change with a community mental health–focused activity or through peer support. These features typically fall into the following categories:

- **Knowledge:** what patrons know about a mental health–related topic—for example, warning signs of a mental health crisis, suicide risk factors, or the availability of local resources
- **Beliefs and attitudes:** what patrons think or feel about mental health topics or people with mental illness—for example, your goal could be about reducing the stigma of mental illness or of help-seeking
- **Behaviors and behavioral intentions:** what patrons do or would be willing to do in certain situations—for example, willingness to reach out for support, if needed, or willingness to reach out to others who might need support
- **Conditions or experiences:** patrons' specific experiences or symptoms—for example, your goal could relate to reducing social isolation or increasing social support.

A goal statement should not focus on implementing a specific activity or program. It should be about creating change for a specific target population in one of the categories previously listed.

The two simplest approaches to writing a goal statement are the following:

1. **Reverse your problem statement.** Essentially, write the opposite of the problem.
2. **Finish the sentence**, "We will know we are succeeding when . . ."

An example of using these approaches when writing a goal statement is as follows:

- **Example problem.** Spanish-speaking older adults are experiencing high rates of loneliness and isolation.
  - **Example goal (approach 1).** Spanish-speaking older adults experience low rates of loneliness and isolation.
  - **Example goal (approach 2).** [We will know we are succeeding when] Spanish-speaking older adults have strong social support and community connections.

To make the goal SMART, add in the *specific* and *time-bound* components, as follows:

- **Example goal.** One year after implementation, Spanish-speaking older adults who participate in our library's L4H senior programming will report having significantly increased social support and community connections.

Once you have developed your L4H goals, move on to Chapter 5 to select the specific activities you wish to implement as part of L4H in your library.

Worksheet: Setting SMART Goals

To set your own SMART goal, start by answering these key questions:

1. What problem do your needs data point to?
2. What are you trying to accomplish?
3. Who is the target population?

Write your problem statement in one sentence:

Now, reverse the problem statement, or complete this phrase:

"We will know we are succeeding when . . ."

Finally, make your goal SMART by adding in specific and time-bound components:

"I think that Libraries for Health is a great initiative because we can bring health to a central location where people will come, especially when there's nothing else in the area, because truly there is nothing else in this area."

Garfield Libraries peer specialist

CHAPTER 5

Topics covered in this chapter:

- Selecting mental health activities for your library
- Assessing the fit with your library context
- Finding a peer specialist

Resources included:

- Tip Sheet: Recruiting a Peer Specialist Who Meets Your Needs
- Tip Sheet: Where to Find Effective Mental Health Support and Education Activities
- Tip Sheet: Examples of Evidence-Based Mental Health Programs for Libraries
- Worksheet: Fit Assessment Tool

Peer Specialist and Activity Selection

The L4H pilot components consisted of a peer specialist, mental health programming, and external partnerships. These are adaptable to different library needs and contexts, and exactly how they are implemented in your library will be up to you and the availability of resources and capacity.

This chapter focuses on finding a peer specialist and identifying appropriate mental health programming. It will help you decide—from the activities you are considering—which are a good fit with your library, which are feasible to implement, and which might require additional resources or are not feasible to implement at the moment. Additionally, this chapter will help you assess the fit of the activity and your capacity to implement it.

Finding a Peer Specialist

Hiring and onboarding your peer specialist will likely occur after you have secured necessary funding and built appropriate partnerships, but you can begin your search before your resources are in place. There are different types of peer specialists, including those who specialize in substance use and addiction, trauma, grief, caregiving, and parenting. Depending on your local community, you might want to search for peer specialists who speak languages spoken by your target populations or who identify with specific populations (for example, disability, LGBTQ+, or veteran communities). Tailor your peer specialist search to the needs and goals you defined in Chapter 4, and, if possible, search for individuals with those specific experiences or skills in those areas.

We recommend that libraries actively engage in this process because finding someone who is the right fit for your community might take some time. If your library plans to hire a peer specialist directly (and potentially partner with a peer support training or supervision organization), consider recruiting from library staff or volunteers. Libraries in the L4H pilot program found it particularly effective to have a peer specialist who was already familiar with or a member of the library community, in terms of building trust among the patron community.

The Copeland Center also offers a resource to locate organizations (1) that train and oversee peer specialists and (2) with whom you can partner to hire a peer specialist from within its organization. If you are partnering with an outside peer support organization, we recommend working closely with them to ensure that the peer specialist's interests, background, and skills align with your library's needs and goals. To learn more about peer specialists in your state—including potential funding sources, statewide certification agencies and requirements, information on supervision or joint supervision, and peer support trainings—and to find a peer support organization, visit the Copeland Center's Peer Specialist Database (https://copelandcenter.com/doors-wellbeing/peer-specialist-database) (Copeland Center for Wellness and Recovery, undated).

Peer Support Certification

As noted in Chapter 2, peer specialists in the L4H pilot were certified in the state of Texas. Choosing between a certified and a noncertified peer specialist involves weighing several pros and cons. Certified peer specialists have obtained standardized training, ensuring that they possess essential skills and knowledge, which enhances their credibility and fosters trust among patrons and mental health professionals. Certified peer specialists are often required to engage in ongoing professional development, which keeps them updated on best practices. In some states, certified peer specialists are reimbursable through Medicaid. However, certification, if not reimbursed, can be costly and time-consuming to achieve, and choosing only among those who are certified might limit the potential pool of available peer specialists. On the other hand, noncertified peer specialists offer flexibility and might be more cost-effective; considering individuals without certification might broaden the pool of candidates and allow your library to bring diverse life experiences and perspectives that can enrich support roles. Yet noncertified individuals might lack formal training, which can lead to variability in the quality of support, and they might face challenges in establishing credibility without recognized qualifications. Ultimately, libraries should consider their specific needs and resources and the communities they aim to serve when making this decision (see the following tip sheet).

Tip Sheet: Recruiting a Peer Specialist Who Meets Your Needs

Consider the skills and expertise you hope a peer specialist will bring to your library and let these goals guide your efforts to recruit and hire a peer specialist. Focus on the needs and goals identified in Chapter 4, as well as the barriers faced by patrons. Think about the following:

- **Match between peer specialist skills and planned activities.** Do you hope your peer specialist will primarily support patrons in one-on-one meetings? Plan and execute events or group programs? Connect the library with other community resources? Consider whether the peer specialist's background and skills are a good match for your library's goals.
- **Topics.** Peer specialists focus on different topic areas or mental health challenges that align with their interests and lived experience (e.g., with addiction and recovery, depression, or other topics). If your library's goals focus on specific mental health topics, you might want to seek out peer specialists with that expertise.
- **Language.** You might wish to seek peer specialists who share linguistic and cultural backgrounds with your target population.
- **Expectations, reporting structures, and logistics.** Set clear expectations for supervision, communication, and library support for the peer specialist's work. How many hours will the peer specialist need to be in the library? Is travel expected? Is there an ability to work remotely (i.e., telehealth)? How and to whom should the peer specialist communicate about scheduling conflicts, questions, and concerns? What mandated requirements are in place for library employees (e.g., background checks, substance use screenings)?
- **Familiarity with the library and community.** Peer specialists do not need to be external hires. Consider whether any existing library staff or volunteers would be interested in getting trained and certified to provide peer support and how their job descriptions and responsibilities could shift to adopt this new role. Also, consider asking any partner organizations for recommendations.

"We have [patrons] that only speak Spanish. So that has been a huge help [to have a Spanish-speaking peer specialist] because it's one thing to put something in a Google Doc and just translate it or Google Translate. It's another to have someone come in and be like, how's your day going? And you can chit chat with them in their language."

L4H library director

Keep in mind that although peer specialists are trained in mental health topics, libraries might be a new setting for them. Make a plan for how you will train and support your peer specialist so they can thrive in your library. If possible, designate a staff person to help integrate the peer specialist into the library, provide general supervision, and champion their efforts. Part of this will include educating your staff about the peer specialist role, so they know what to expect as well. Refer to the "Peer Specialist Roles: Do's and Don'ts" tip sheet in Chapter 2 to help set expectations.

Selecting Mental Health Activities

Once you have assessed the mental health needs in your community and set goals, you will want to select and plan activities to help attain those goals. We recommend choosing activities with demonstrated evidence of their effectiveness for the impact you are aiming to achieve. Look for activities and programs that have been studied in other settings or are otherwise recognized as promising or best practices.

In Chapter 2, we covered the different types of activities that might be helpful to implement, including patron engagement activities, mental health support, education activities, and efforts to enhance resources and circulation materials. Although engagement activities and resource enhancements are important complementary activities in L4H, peer support and mental health support and education activities are the program's core evidence-based elements. Therefore, in this section, we focus on suggestions for evidence-based or promising mental health support and education activities that can be implemented in libraries.

The first tip sheet in this section includes registries of effective interventions that can be filtered by topic and target population. The second tip sheet includes examples of evidence-based or promising practices to address some of the common target populations and goals that were identified by libraries in the L4H pilot. We have included those activities with the most flexibility in facilitation—that is, those that could be provided by peer specialists, staff, or other individuals with minimal training or expertise requirements. These activities also might be widely available from trained providers for a nominal cost.

Use the following tip sheets to locate activities to implement in your libraries that will help you meet your needs and goals.

Tip Sheet: Where to Find Effective Mental Health Support and Education Activities

We highly recommend that libraries implement activities that have some evidence supporting their effectiveness. Evidence-based practice registries curate information about research-based programs and include effectiveness ratings for different interventions. These interventions can be filtered by topic area (e.g., stress, parenting, sleep) and by target population or age group.

Registry	Description	Source
Pennsylvania State University's Clearinghouse for Military Family Readiness	Despite its name, this resource is not just for military families. The clearinghouse includes a comprehensive registry of programs for children, adults, and families designed to prevent and address common social and behavioral health issues. Use the filter function to search for programs for different populations or to address specific topics, such as parenting, suicide prevention, anxiety, depression, and substance use. Programs are rated on a continuum from effective to ineffective.	https://www.continuum.militaryfamilies.psu.edu/search (Clearinghouse for Military Family Readiness, undated)
SAMHSA's Evidence-Based Practice Resource Center	The Evidence-Based Practice Resource Center is a clearinghouse for evidence-based tools and resources. You can search for information by topic area (including mental health) and target audience (including community organizations).	https://www.samhsa.gov/resource-search/ebp (SAMHSA, undated-b)
Blueprints for Healthy Youth Development	Blueprints is a registry that identifies and promotes evidence-based programs designed to prevent antisocial behavior and promote positive youth development. The registry includes only programs that are "promising" or considered "model" programs, meaning that they have a minimum level of effectiveness.	https://www.blueprintsprograms.org/program-search/ (Blueprints for Healthy Youth Development, undated)
Suicide Prevention Resource Center	The Suicide Prevention Resource Center includes an online library of programs, toolkits, and trainings designed to prevent suicide.	https://sprc.org (Suicide Prevention Resource Center, undated)
NAMI	NAMI produces educational materials and provides trainings and resources designed to improve the lives of individuals with mental illness. To find programs and trainings near you, search for your local NAMI affiliate on the website.	https://www.nami.org/support-education/mental-health-education/ (NAMI, undated-b)
California Evidence-Based Clearinghouse	The California Evidence-Based Clearinghouse is a database that provides information on programs, practices, and interventions related to child welfare and family well-being. You can search by topic area, intended outcomes, delivery setting, and other areas.	https://www.cebc4cw.org/registry/ (California Evidence-Based Clearinghouse, undated)
The Community Toolbox	If you did not find a program or activity to suit your needs in the resources listed above, the Center for Community Health and Development at the University of Kansas Community Toolbox curates an extensive list of registries for evidence-based programs and best practices.	https://ctb.ku.edu/en/databases-best-practices (Community Tool Box, undated)

Tip Sheet: Examples of Evidence-Based Mental Health Programs for Libraries

This tip sheet covers two types of mental health–related programming that libraries could implement: (1) programs that train library staff to be more effective and confident in their everyday interactions with patrons who are experiencing mental health problems and (2) programs that train partner organizations or library staff to deliver programming directly to patrons in the library (e.g., in the form of weekly groups or workshops).

Type of Programming	Program	Purpose	Further Reading
Training for library staff	Mental Health First Aid	Reduce mental health stigma among library staff. Increase staff's knowledge and skills that relate to identifying and responding to patrons with mental health concerns.	https://www.mentalhealthfirstaid.org/ (Mental Health First Aid, undated)
	Applied Suicide Intervention Skills Training (ASIST)	Increase library staff's ability to recognize risk factors for suicide and to intervene with individuals experiencing suicidal thoughts and behaviors.	https://www.samhsa.gov/resource/dbhis/applied-suicide-intervention-skills-training-asist (SAMHSA, undated-a)
	Motivational interviewing	Improve library staff's skills in how to talk about problematic thoughts and behaviors with patrons in a way that promotes motivation to change.	https://www.mentalhealthfirstaid.org/ (Mental Health First Aid, undated
Program for patrons	Behavioral activation	Prevent or reduce depression.	https://div12.org/treatment/behavioral-activation-for-depression/ (Society of Clinical Psychology, undated)
	Parenting classes (e.g., 1-2-3 Magic, The Incredible Years, Triple P)	Improve parenting skills.	https://www.123magic.com (1-2-3 Magic, undated) https://www.incredibleyears.com/early-intervention-programs/parents (The Incredible Years, undated) https://www.triplep.net/glo-en/home/ (Triple P Positive Parenting Program, undated)
	Relaxation, mindfulness, and meditation training	Reduce negative effects of stress, anxiety, and tension. Increase concentration and overall well-being.	https://www.nccih.nih.gov/health/relaxation-techniques-what-you-need-to-know (National Center for Complementary and Integrative Health, undated)

Worksheet:
Fit Assessment Tool

Complete this worksheet for each activity under consideration and review the adaptations needed to help you decide which to implement and which to reject. Look at the number of no's and consider the extent of the adaptations. For the activities you decide to implement, the adaptations noted in the right-hand column will become part of your workplan in Chapter 6.

Does the activity fit with the . . .	**Yes/no**	**What adaptations, if any, need to be made to improve the fit?**
Target population • Identified needs • Demographics (e.g., age, language, culture) • Other important characteristics (e.g., education level, work schedules)	Y ☐ N ☐	
Library • Organizational priorities • Current programming • Schedule • Other important characteristics (e.g., building layout, space availability)	Y ☐ N ☐	
Community • Cultural norms and values • Other important characteristics (e.g., rural or urban, United States or international)	Y ☐ N ☐	

Assessing Fit

For each activity under consideration, you should think about how closely the goals and activities match with the goals and needs identified for your target population. There might be small changes you can make to activities to optimize the fit and enhance effectiveness. That said, be cautious when adjusting an evidence-based strategy. Small changes—such as adjusting wording or materials to better appeal to your audience, updating statistics or customizing them to your context, changing visuals, or adding small components to activities—might help improve the relevance of the activity for your audience. However, altering the program or activity substantially could render it ineffective. Substantial changes would include removing whole pieces of curriculum, shortening trainings, changing the topic entirely, or implementing the activity with a completely different target population (for example, implementing an intervention that was developed for seniors within a teen population). Where possible, consult with the developers of the intervention or other experts if you need to make any substantial changes.

Once you have a rough sense of the activities you would like to include as part of L4H, proceed to Chapter 6.

SALUD
MENTAL EN
MENTAL
HEALTH IN
SAN MARCOS
Directory of services
available in and around our
community.
Everyone needs help
sometime.

CHAPTER 6

Topics covered in this chapter:

- Creating a workplan
- Building partnerships
- Funding peer support and mental health activities
- Launching L4H

Resources included:

- Worksheet: Implementation Workplan
- Worksheet: Preparing for Effective Collaboration
- Tip Sheet: Options for Funding Peer Support and Mental Health Activities

Prepare and Launch

This chapter outlines steps your library can take to create a workplan, develop partnerships, secure funding, and launch and implement L4H. This chapter also provides a customizable sample workplan, to help plan the tasks needed to effectively launch and implement mental health activities in your library. In addition, this chapter will advise on how to establish effective collaborative partnerships, including with peer support organizations, local mental health resources, and others interested in implementing L4H activities. Funding options for L4H activities are also covered.

Creating a Workplan

The first step in getting ready to launch is to create a detailed workplan for the activities you intend to implement. The following worksheet provides an example format, which includes tasks organized by topic and spaces to assign staff and note the due date. Workplans are most effective when tasks are clearly defined, are assigned to an individual, have a deadline, and are revisited often and kept updated. For your first iteration of the workplan, you might not have a peer specialist in place or all of the implementation staff identified just yet; as you onboard a peer specialist or involve new staff in implementation, work closely with them to delineate these tasks.

Worksheet: Implementation Workplan

Tasks	Person Assigned	Due Date
Preparation		
Gather data on the mental health needs in your community (use Chapter 4's checklist)		
Review the "Identifying and Prioritizing Community Needs and Resources" worksheet		
Review the "Setting SMART Goals" worksheet		
Other:		
Stakeholder engagement		
Generate list of local community service organizations and providers		
Contact those working on issues that surfaced in your needs assessment		
Engage staff to build buy-in		
Complete the "Preparing for Effective Collaboration" worksheet		
Other:		
Funding		
Create a budget		
Work with partner organizations to identify and apply for joint funding opportunities or leverage their existing funding		
Research potential funding opportunities and apply for grants		
Other:		
Peer specialist recruitment and hiring		
Research peer support organizations in your area		
Contract with a peer support organization or recruit a peer specialist directly (if hiring directly, make sure that proper training, certification, and supervision are in place)		
Onboard peer specialist		
Set roles and expectations		
Set up space in library for peer specialist		
Set schedule for regular (e.g., weekly) check-ins to monitor progress and support the peer specialist's integration into the library		
Other:		

Tasks	Person Assigned	Due Date
Materials and resources		
Purchase any materials and resources, including curriculum, equipment, and promotional or other items needed to implement the activity		
Secure space needed for the activity		
Other:		
Advertising		
Draft event signage		
Draft newsletter announcement		
Plan social media announcement		
Create targeted emails and announcements for community partners and collaborators		
Other:		
Evaluation and continuous quality improvement		
Design evaluation tools (e.g., survey, focus group, feedback form)		
Recruit participants		
Collect data (e.g., conduct field survey, lead focus groups, conduct interviews)		
Analyze results		
Other:		

Building Partnerships

Organizational partnerships are key to the success and sustainability of L4H. We recommend pursuing partnerships with peer support organizations, local community services organizations, academic institutions, other library-cohort implementation partners, your local city government, and Friends of the Library and other nonprofit support organizations.

Peer support organizations, such as those you might encounter during your efforts to recruit a peer specialist (Chapter 5), are likely to be invaluable partners for helping to recruit, train, certify, and supervise your peer specialist. These organizations can take on the work of managing the peer specialist and ensuring that they are supported and effective in their work. They might also be attuned to grant opportunities in your area, through which you could fund your peer specialist position.

Where **mental health providers and social services** exist in your region, you might seek out opportunities to refer patrons in need to those services or provide information about the service availability to patrons. Those organizations might be interested in providing pamphlets or flyers, participating in resource fairs or programs at your library, hosting representatives from different community organizations as service access points, or even colocating a service in your library.

One specific form of partnership that can be beneficial is a **learning cohort**. Libraries in the L4H pilot participated in a learning cohort. Made up of library directors, the cohort met quarterly to discuss shared experiences, challenges, and solutions. The cohort also participated in mental health–related trainings that gave cohort members tools to be responsive to patrons and manage their own stressful experiences. Many library directors reported that this was one of the most valuable aspects of their L4H experience, and they developed strong relationships with other libraries that expanded beyond the scope of L4H. Although replicating the cohort of the L4H pilot libraries might be unfeasible, finding at least one partner library to exchange ideas with might be feasible. You might want to reach out to members of your professional network to see whether other libraries are interested in implementing mental health programming and whether they would be interested in connecting at a regular cadence to exchange ideas.

Academic partnerships can significantly enhance mental health efforts by providing access to research and expertise from universities and colleges. Collaborating with academic institutions, especially departments focused on social work, psychology, and public health, can offer valuable insights and evidence-based strategies for addressing mental health challenges. These partnerships also can create internship and volunteer opportunities, allowing students to support library programs while gaining practical experience. Additionally, academic collaborations can lead to joint research projects and funding opportunities, enabling libraries to implement and evaluate innovative mental health interventions. By leveraging these partnerships, libraries can strengthen their role as community hubs for mental health support and education.

Building partnerships with your **city or local government** can significantly enhance the implementation and sustainability of your efforts. Such collaborations can provide libraries with access to additional resources, funding opportunities, and policy support that are crucial for embedding mental health supports. Local government agencies often have a vested interest in promoting community well-being and can assist in aligning library initiatives with broader public health goals. By partnering with city officials, libraries can gain valuable insights into community needs and priorities, facilitating more-targeted and more-effective mental health programming. Additionally, these partnerships can open doors to shared spaces, joint events, and colocation opportunities, further integrating libraries into the community fabric. Engaging with local government can also enhance the visibility and credibility of library programs, fostering community trust and participation. Through these collaborative efforts, libraries can strengthen their role as essential community resources, advancing both mental health and overall community resilience.

Finally, working with your local **Friends of the Library** and similar nonprofit organizations can significantly enhance your impact and reach. These groups, composed of dedicated supporters and volunteers, offer critical advocacy, fundraising, and community engagement. By collaborating with them, libraries can mobilize resources, organize events, secure donations, and increase awareness for mental health programs. Their connections with local businesses and leaders open additional partnership opportunities, strengthening the library's capacity to implement L4H effectively. Leveraging their enthusiasm and commitment enhances the library's role as a vital community hub for mental health and well-being.

We recommend continuously working to build and maintain any partnerships that you pursue. They might not come together in the order we lay out, and they might require ongoing outreach and communication to maintain. When you identify potential partners, we recommend discussing goals for the program early on to make sure that the partnership is a good match. Be sure that both parties understand (1) what each will do as part of the partnership and (2) how information and feedback will be shared with each other. The following collaboration worksheet offers some guiding questions to discuss with potential partners.

Worksheet: Preparing for Effective Collaboration

Discuss the following questions with each potential partner organization:

- What does each organization hope to accomplish through L4H?
- What are the most important resources each organization can bring to the partnership?
- What potential challenges does each organization see in partnering?
- How does each organization envision working together to plan and implement tasks associated with L4H?
- How do partners envision sharing information, and how often should they meet to discuss implementation tasks, challenges, or opportunities?

Guiding Questions	Partner Organization 1	Partner Organization 2
What does each organization hope to accomplish through L4H?		
What are the most important resources each organization can bring to the partnership?		
What potential challenges does each organization see in partnering?		
How does each organization envision working together to plan and implement tasks associated with L4H?		
How do partners envision sharing information, and how often should they meet to discuss implementation tasks, challenges, or opportunities?		

Funding Peer Support and Mental Health Activities

Although some L4H activities can be done for free or at a low cost by leveraging partnerships and donations of time and talents, most L4H activities will require some financial investment. Costs could include paying peer specialists and facilitators of external trainings or activities, purchasing new mental health–related collections and other materials, and advertising L4H programs. The following tip sheet offers some ideas for funding options.

Tip Sheet: Options for Funding Peer Support and Mental Health Activities

There are several options to fund peer support (including any necessary training, certification, and supervision) and mental health activities in your library. Consider the following:

- Work with community partners to identify shared grant opportunities and leverage complementary resources.
- Contact local businesses to ask whether they might be able to donate funds to cover supplies or funding for mental health programming.
- Contact organizations that train and supervise peer specialists. Many of these organizations have grants or grant-writing abilities and might be looking for community organizations in which to embed peer support.
- Employ a peer specialist through your library or city budget.
- Train library staff to provide peer support. If you go this route, be sure to consider ways to appropriately adjust library staff's job descriptions and workloads.
- Obtain grants from foundations or government organizations to fund peer specialists or other mental health programming. Start by exploring
  - Foundation Directory: https://fconline.foundationcenter.org (Candid, undated-a)
  - Grants.gov: https://www.grants.gov (Grants.gov, undated)
  - GrantStation: https://grantstation.com (GrantStation, undated)
  - GuideStar: https://www.guidestar.org (Candid, undated-b)
  - Philanthropy News Digest: https://philanthropynewsdigest.org (Candid, undated-c).
- Tip: HRSA and SAMHSA are two federal funders that have supported mental health programming, including peer support.

You likely also have connections with grantmakers and community foundations that support state and local nonprofits. We suggest that you explore what support they can offer.

Once your resources are in place, we recommend collaboratively refining program goals and developing a more detailed workplan for program implementation. The next section of this chapter covers this preparation phase, which will include ensuring that necessary stakeholders, such as library leadership and staff, are on board.

"Individuals involved in planning L4H activities included the library director, library staff, with the focus on the programming librarians. There has been some input certainly from the professionals that we have hired, but also from the community members who most commonly come and access these programs."

L4H library staff member

Launching

When launching mental health activities at your library, consider the timing of your launch, ways to advertise the new offerings, and whether a kickoff event would encourage engagement among community members.

Timing. When planning the launch of mental health activities at your library, timing is a crucial factor to ensure maximum impact and community engagement. Aligning the kickoff with national awareness events, such as Mental Health Month in May and National Recovery Month in September, can provide a strategic advantage by tapping into existing public interest and media coverage. Additionally, consider the library's programming schedule to avoid conflicts with other major events and ensure that staff and resources are available. Launching at the beginning of the academic year or after the winter holidays can also be effective, as these periods often coincide with heightened stress and a renewed focus on personal well-being. Understanding the community's calendar, including local events and cultural observances, can further inform the best timing for the kickoff.

Advertising. A comprehensive communication and marketing strategy will help you best reach your target populations. Use multiple channels at your disposal to disseminate information, including social media platforms, the library's website, newsletters, patrons themselves, and community bulletin boards. Ensure that your messaging is easy to understand and provided in languages spoken by your patron community. For some, mental health topics might be intimidating or even taboo; work closely with your mental health partner organizations and/or peer specialist to be sure that your messaging is inclusive and welcoming for your community. Working through your governing agency's communication channels might be particularly effective because the agency might have a broad reach and communications expertise. Craft clear, engaging messages that highlight the benefits and objectives of the mental health program and highlight the new offerings at your library. Partner with local media outlets for press releases and interviews to broaden the reach. Collaborating with local mental health organizations can enhance credibility and extend outreach efforts. Additionally, consider hosting a pre-launch information session or webinar to generate interest and provide potential participants with a preview of the activities and resources that will be available.

"[The local school district], [our library,] and several other community organizations hosted a 'summer programs and resources' kickoff event. Over 500 people of all ages participated to learn about summer feeding, summer reading, the [paratransit service] Care-A-Van, and other health resources. The event was held at [a local] park, which attracted an audience that has a demonstrated need for these resources."

L4H library progress report

Kickoff events. Consider planning a kickoff event or series of events. Kickoff events should be designed to foster engagement, education, and community-building. Consider hosting a mental health fair or a local community-resource fair that features booths from local mental health organizations, offering resources and information to attendees. This is a great way to introduce your peer specialist to the community and begin building trust and familiarity with them.

A library open-house night can also be a great way to introduce new mental health–related offerings to the community. Invite guest speakers, such as mental health professionals and individuals with lived experiences who can share insights and personal stories, and offer previews of new activities, circulation materials, and peer support offerings. Providing light refreshments and creating a welcoming atmosphere can further encourage participation. The goal is to create an inclusive, supportive environment that both educates and empowers community members to prioritize their mental health.

"For me, it's a place to go. So I don't isolate, so I don't get depressed, and I have purpose here in my life. And it's only a few miles from my house, and that's important, living in a rural place, to have some place to go."

Jarrell Community Library volunteer

CHAPTER 7

Topics covered in this chapter:

- Improving L4H as you implement
- Sustaining L4H over time

Resources included:

- Tip Sheet: Key Improvement Process Elements
- Tip Sheet: Strategies to Effectively Communicate Your Success

Improvements and Sustainability

This chapter is focused on processes that can help libraries improve and sustain their L4H programming over time. These can include ways to continuously evaluate program implementation and outcomes so that libraries can change and adapt the program as community needs, staff capacity, funding, and other factors evolve.

Improving Libraries for Health

Although a full discussion of evaluation and analysis is beyond the scope of this toolkit, libraries can set up processes early on to (1) monitor progress and (2) collect information to guide their implementation efforts and any needed adjustments to programming.

"The library collects data by staff members documenting the number of attendees at programs, results from surveys and connecting with patrons to see what additional resources the library can provide to continue meeting their specific needs. After reviewing this collected feedback and information, within the last six months, our program attendee numbers have doubled."

L4H library progress report

Many organizations use an approach called the plan-do-study-act (PDSA) method to help evaluate program changes (Agency for Healthcare Research and Quality, 2024). This is a relatively straightforward strategy that involves four basic steps:

1. Specify the program or change you are seeking to make, your objective for that change, and the steps involved (*plan*).
2. Implement the change and document how it went (*do*).
3. Analyze the process and outcome in terms of whether your objective(s) were met and any lessons learned (*study*).
4. Draw conclusions and determine your next action steps (*act*).

The PDSA cycle can be repeated over time as your program evolves. The Agency for Healthcare Research and Quality provides helpful guidance for organizations interested in using this approach (https://www.ahrq.gov/health-literacy/improve/precautions/tool2b.html) (Agency for Healthcare Research and Quality, 2024).

Another approach is RAND's GTO (Chinman, Imm, and Wandersman, 2004), an evidence-based, ten-step process for implementing and continuously improving behavioral health–related programming, such as L4H. The GTO website provides helpful guidance, worksheets, and other materials: https://www.rand.org/health-care/projects/getting-to-outcomes.html (RAND Corporation, undated). As mentioned in the introduction, this toolkit is modeled after the GTO process.

Both PDSA cycles and GTO can be helpful resources to augment this toolkit as libraries determine how to monitor and adapt their implementation of L4H. Regardless of which tool your library selects, however, there are three critical elements to include in your improvement process: reevaluation of community needs and program goals, analysis and evaluation of program success metrics, and adjustment of the implementation plan. The following tip sheet describes these elements in greater detail.

For other examples of evaluation metrics, we recommend reviewing the L4H evaluation report, which includes information about the measures used to evaluate the implementation of the L4H pilot. This report will be available at www.rand.org in summer 2025 (Ayer et al., 2025).

Tip Sheet: Key Improvement Process Elements

Reevaluation of community needs and program goals. Community needs are not stagnant and might change. Even if these needs do not change, libraries might want to periodically reevaluate their goals to ensure that they are continuing to align with their community needs. It is also important for libraries to keep an eye on the future and anticipate potential shifts in need. Regularly review the data sources in the "Sources of Information on Community Needs" tip sheet in Chapter 4. Update your workplan as you go, adjusting for new information.

Analysis and evaluation of program success metrics. Whether working internally or with an external partner, libraries should be monitoring the SMART goals that they set at the beginning, to determine the success of their programs and activities. This is an imperative step that allows libraries to invest in what is working and adjust for what is not. Examples of information and metrics that libraries might wish to collect include program attendance, staff well-being or burnout, changes in issuance of new library cards, and patron satisfaction. You can ask questions like:

- Have things gone according to plan?
- What adjustments did you need to make, and were they effective?
- What did participants like or dislike, and what did they state as barriers to participating in activities or engaging with your peer specialist?

Adjustment of the implementation plan. Take the insights gained from the initial planning and implementation phases to make changes in your library's ongoing implementation plan. Use the information gathered to identify potential barriers and areas for improvement and to make informed adjustments to your activities. Consider adopting new technologies (e.g., potentially providing peer support or programming via video conferencing), reallocating resources to activities that were the most effective, or refining service-delivery methods to better meet patron needs (e.g., trying to reach patrons outside the library, in other community settings). This iterative process will help ensure that services remain aligned with patron needs.

Sustaining Libraries for Health over Time

This section provides guidance on how to keep a successful L4H program going, even after the initial funding has ended.

Demonstrate and Communicate Effectiveness

If you have been heeding the advice in this guide, your library has been collecting data on its L4H program since inception. You used data to assess your community's needs and determine how to design your L4H program, and you have been monitoring program implementation to measure its success and determine whether changes need to be made to strengthen its impact. Sharing highlights from your data to demonstrate your program's impact (see the following tip sheet) can help garner support and enthusiasm for sustaining a successful program. The more your community knows about your program and its positive impact, the stronger support will be for its sustainment.

Tip Sheet: Strategies to Effectively Communicate Your Success

- Consider a multimode approach to reach diverse audiences. Examples include
  - printed materials (e.g., newsletters, flyers, brochures)
  - social media
  - traditional media (e.g., local newspapers, television)
  - presentations to community partners, funders, and other local organizations (e.g., mental health advocacy groups, veteran service organizations)
  - word of mouth (e.g., library patrons, neighbors, colleagues, friends, family)
  - the library website.
- Include quotes from program participants or staff. If you do not have quotes yet, ask individuals who had good experiences with the program to provide testimonials that you can use in your communications (anonymized, if needed).
- Emphasize the continued need for your program in your community. Share information from your community needs assessment (if available) and/or from public data sources. In addition, information collected by your library, such as the number of new patrons, program attendance, and results from satisfaction surveys, can be important sources of evidence of need for the program.
- Develop your "elevator pitch" to explain your program and share how it helped your library and community. This should be a short (less than one minute) explanation.
  - **Example elevator pitch:**

    Welcome to "Mindful Library," where mental health support is seamlessly integrated into our local library. Our program offers free access to mental health peer specialists, providing workshops and resources tailored to our community's needs. By partnering with local organizations, we ensure timely, compassionate care in a familiar setting. We also train library staff to recognize and respond to mental health issues, fostering a supportive and inclusive environment for all patrons. Join us in transforming our library into a beacon of community wellness, in which every visit promotes mental well-being.

"We are forming partnerships and determining which of the programs have had the greatest impact. With a combination of partnerships, additional grants, and city funding—we expect to maintain a source of mental health services to our community."

L4H library progress report

Program Champions

An influential program advocate or champion can make all the difference in whether your program is sustained. The program champion should be someone with decisionmaking power and influential connections either inside or outside the library. This could be someone internal to the library (such as the director) or an external person (such as a city council member, county commissioner, or another respected community leader). This person should be able to clearly communicate details of the program and discuss why it is important to library staff and to community members, leaders, and funders.

Training and Staff Retention

Staff turnover can be a major challenge in sustaining new programs. The time and resources required to frequently hire and train new staff can be costly and disruptive. Although some staff turnover is to be expected and is a sign of organizational health (because periodically infusing new ideas and energy into a workplace is important), frequent turnover—especially in leadership positions—can make it very difficult to maintain consistent, high-quality programming. Library staff might be experiencing burnout in addition to everyday life stressors. Ensuring that staff are equipped with the skills needed to manage those stressors can help mitigate burnout and, potentially, staff turnover. In addition, library staff should receive high-quality training in your L4H program and their specific role so that they can feel confident in their ability to support program implementation. Training should include more than just a one-time event; staff should have easy access to ongoing supervision and coaching for troubleshooting and developing and refining their skills.

Funding

Although funding has been covered in previous chapters, it will come as no surprise that additional funding will be key to program sustainment. Periodically reviewing your data for insights into program components—and the costs associated with those components—can help you to decide which components to seek funding for. Some libraries might be fortunate to receive a steady and predictable stream of funding from their state or local government; others might be regularly making pitches and writing proposals to fund their programs. If your library is seeking funding on a regular basis, your networking and communication efforts will be a major asset. In addition, you can search for funding opportunities online. Refer to the "Options for Funding Peer Support and Mental Health Activities" tip sheet in Chapter 6.

CHAPTER 8

Conclusion

This toolkit underscores the vital role libraries can play in enhancing community mental health. By integrating evidence-based mental health supports, libraries can transform into pivotal community hubs that not only provide access to information but also foster well-being and resilience. The L4H pilot program demonstrated the profound impact libraries can have when they embrace mental health initiatives, offering a blueprint for success that other libraries can replicate. Through careful planning, community engagement, and strategic partnerships, libraries can address critical mental health needs, reduce stigma, and provide accessible support to all patrons. As trusted and welcoming spaces, libraries have a unique opportunity to bridge gaps in mental health care and become beacons of hope and support in their communities. By leveraging the insights and strategies outlined in this toolkit, libraries can continue to evolve and meet the ever-changing needs of their patrons, ensuring a healthier, more connected community for all.

Abbreviations

GTO	Getting To Outcomes™
HRSA	Health Resources and Services Administration
L4H	Libraries for Health
LGBTQ+	lesbian, gay, bisexual, transgender, queer–plus
NAMI	National Alliance on Mental Illness
PDSA	plan-do-study-act
SAMHSA	Substance Abuse and Mental Health Services Administration
SDF	St. David's Foundation
SMART	specific, measurable, achievable, relevant, time-bound

References

1-2-3 Magic, homepage, undated. As of January 30, 2025:
https://www.123magic.com/

Agency for Healthcare Research and Quality, "Health Literacy Universal Precautions Toolkit, 3rd Edition," webpage, last updated March 2024. As of January 31, 2025:
https://www.ahrq.gov/health-literacy/improve/precautions/tool2b.html

Arnaez, James Marcus, Anne C. Krendl, Bryan P. McCormick, Zhongxue Chen, and Andrea K. Chomistek, "The Association of Depression Stigma with Barriers to Seeking Mental Health Care: A Cross-Sectional Analysis," *Journal of Mental Health*, Vol. 29, No. 2, 2020.

Ayer, Lynsay, Karen Christianson, Ivy Todd, Logan Dick, Amy L. Shearer, Yoselín Mayoral, Abigail Kessler, and Rajeev Ramchand, *Integrating Mental Health Support into Rural Libraries: Evaluation of the Libraries for Health (L4H) Initiative*, RAND Corporation, RR-A3597-1, 2025. As of June 20, 2025:
https://www.rand.org/pubs/research_reports/RRA3597-1.html

Barnett, Miya L., Araceli Gonzalez, Jeanne Miranda, Denise A. Chavira, and Anna S. Lau, "Mobilizing Community Health Workers to Address Mental Health Disparities for Underserved Populations: A Systematic Review," *Administration and Policy in Mental Health,* Vol. 45, No. 2, March 2018.

Blueprints for Healthy Youth Development, "Program Search," webpage, undated. As of November 15, 2024:
https://www.blueprintsprograms.org/program-search/

California Evidence-Based Clearinghouse, "Program Registry," webpage, undated. As of November 15, 2024:
https://www.cebc4cw.org/registry/

Candid, Foundation Directory, homepage, undated-a. As of January 31, 2025:
https://fconline.foundationcenter.org/

Candid, GuideStar, homepage, undated-b. As of January 31, 2025:
https://www.guidestar.org/

Candid, Philanthropy News Digest, homepage, undated-c. As of January 31, 2025:
https://philanthropynewsdigest.org/

Center for Addiction Recovery Support, Peer Recovery Organizations, directory database, undated. As of February 9, 2025:
https://www.carsrecovery.org/resource-directories

Centers for Diseease Control and Prevention, "PLACES: Local Data for Better Health," webpage, undated. As of April 29, 2025:
https://www.cdc.gov/places/

Chinman, Matthew, Pamela Imm, and Abraham Wandersman, *Getting To Outcomes™ 2004: Promoting Accountability Through Methods and Tools for Planning, Implementation, and Evaluation*, RAND Corporation, TR-101-CDC, 2004. As of January 31, 2025:
https://www.rand.org/pubs/technical_reports/TR101.html

Clearinghouse for Military Family Readiness, "Continuum of Evidence: Search Programs," webpage, Pennsylvania State University, undated. As of November 15, 2024:
https://www.continuum.militaryfamilies.psu.edu/search

Community Tool Box, "Databases of Best Practices," webpage, undated. As of November 15, 2024:
https://ctb.ku.edu/en/databases-best-practices

Copeland Center for Wellness and Recovery, Peer Specialist Database, undated. As of January 31, 2025:
https://copelandcenter.com/doors-wellbeing/peer-specialist-database

Gilbert, Michele, Tara Hartnett, G. William Hoagland, Oliver J. Kim, Marilyn Serafini, and Kendall Strong, *Filling the Gaps in the Behavioral Health Workforce*, Bipartisan Policy Center, January 2023.

Grants.gov, homepage, undated. As of January 31, 2025:
https://www.grants.gov/

GrantStation, homepage, undated. As of January 31, 2025:
https://grantstation.com/

Health Resources and Services Administration, "Health Workforce Shortage Areas," webpage, U.S. Department of Health and Human Services, undated. As of November 15, 2024:
https://data.hrsa.gov/topics/health-workforce/shortage-areas

HRSA—*See* Health Resources and Services Administration.

The Incredible Years, "The Incredible Years Series®: Evidence-Based Parenting Programs," webpage, undated. As of January 31, 2025:
https://www.incredibleyears.com/early-intervention-programs/parents

Magidson, Jessica F., Helen E. Jack, Kristen S. Regenauer, and Bronwyn Myers, "Applying Lessons from Task Sharing in Global Mental Health to the Opioid Crisis," *Journal of Consulting and Clinical Psychology*, Vol. 87, No. 10, October 2019.

Mental Health America, County and State Data Map, dashboard, undated. As of January 31, 2025:
https://mhanational.org/mhamapping/mha-state-county-data

Mental Health America Affiliate Resource Center, "Find an Affiliate," webpage, undated. As of January 31, 2025:
https://arc.mhanational.org/find-affiliate

Mental Health First Aid, homepage, National Council for Mental Wellbeing, undated. As of October 24, 2024:
https://www.mentalhealthfirstaid.org/

NAMI—*See* National Alliance on Mental Illness.

National Alliance on Mental Illness, "Find Your Local NAMI," webpage, undated-a. As of January 31, 2025:
https://www.nami.org/findsupport/

National Alliance on Mental Illness, "Mental Health Education," webpage, undated-b. As of January 31, 2025:
https://www.nami.org/support-education/mental-health-education/

National Center for Complementary and Integrative Health, "Relaxation Techniques: What You Need to Know," webpage, National Institutes of Health, undated. As of January 31, 2025:
https://www.nccih.nih.gov/health/relaxation-techniques-what-you-need-to-know

RAND Corporation, "Getting To Outcomes™," webpage, undated. As of January 31, 2025:
https://www.rand.org/health-care/projects/getting-to-outcomes.html

SAMHSA—*See* Substance Abuse and Mental Health Services Administration.

Schnyder, Nina, Radoslaw Panczak, Nicola Groth, and Frauke Schultze-Lutter, "Association Between Mental Health-Related Stigma and Active Help-Seeking: Systematic Review and Meta-Analysis," *British Journal of Psychiatry*, Vol. 210, No. 4, April 2017.

SDF—*See* St. David's Foundation.

Shalaby, Reham A. Hameed, and Vincent I. O. Agyapong, "Peer Support in Mental Health: Literature Review," *JMIR Mental Health*, Vol. 7, No. 6, June 2020.

Snell-Rood, Claire, and Nancy E. Schoenberg, "What Role Can Community Health Workers Play in Connecting Rural Women with Depression to the 'De Facto' Mental Health Care System?" *Community Mental Health Journal*, Vol. 55, No. 5, January 2019.

Society of Clinical Psychology, "Diagnosis: Depression, Treatment: Behavioral Activation for Depression," webpage, Division 12: American Psychological Association, undated. As of January 31, 2025:
https://div12.org/treatment/behavioral-activation-for-depression/

St. David's Foundation, "Libraries for Health," webpage, undated. As of January 31, 2025:
https://stdavidsfoundation.org/how-we-work/grantmaking/what-we-fund/thriving-rural-communities/libraries-for-health/

Substance Abuse and Mental Health Services Administration, "Applied Suicide Intervention Skills Training (ASIST)," webpage, undated-a. As of May 5, 2025:
https://www.samhsa.gov/resource/dbhis/applied-suicide-intervention-skills-training-asist

Substance Abuse and Mental Health Services Administration, "Evidence-Based Practices Resource Center," webpage, undated-b. As of November 15, 2024:
https://www.samhsa.gov/resource-search/ebp

Suicide Prevention Resource Center, homepage, undated. As of January 31, 2025:
https://sprc.org/

Texas Medicaid and Healthcare Partnership, "Peer Specialist Services to Become a Benefit of Texas Medicaid, January 1, 2019," Septempber 9, 2020.

Triple P Positive Parenting Program, homepage, undated. As of January 31, 2025:
https://www.triplep.net/glo-en/home/

U.S. Census Bureau, "Explore Census Data," webpage, undated. As of January 31, 2025:
https://data.census.gov/

www.ingramcontent.com/pod-product-compliance
Ingram Content Group UK Ltd.
Pitfield, Milton Keynes, MK11 3LW, UK
UKHW051339010925
7672UKWH00049B/1126

9 781977 415257